THE HUMAN SPIRIT

Compiled by Kobi Yamada
Designed by Steve Potter and Jenica Wilkie

COMPENDIUM™
PUBLISHING

live inspired.

THIS BOOK IS DEDICATED TO THOSE INDOMITABLE SPIRITS WHO INSPIRE US EVERY DAY.

ACKNOWLEDGEMENTS
These quotations were gathered lovingly but unscientifically over several years and/or contributed by many friends or acquaintances. Some arrived—and survived in our files—on scraps of paper and may therefore be imperfectly worded or attributed. To the authors, contributors and original sources, our thanks, and where appropriate, our apologies. —The editors

WITH SPECIAL THANKS TO
Jason Aldrich, Gerry Baird, Jay Baird, Neil Beaton, Doug Cruickshank, Jim Darragh, Kari & Kyle Diercks, Josie & Rob Estes, Jennifer Hurwitz, Liam Lavery, Connie McMartin, Cristal & Brad Olberg, Janet Potter & Family, Aimee Rawlins, Diane Roger, Sam Sundquist, Drew Wilkie, Robert & Mary Anne Wilkie, Heidi & Shale Yamada, Justi, Tote & Caden Yamada, Robert & Val Yamada, Kaz & Kristin Yamada, Tai & Joy Yamada, Anne Zadra, August & Arline Zadra, Gus & Rosie Zadra and Dan Zadra.

CREDITS
Compiled By Kobi Yamada
Designed By Steve Potter & Jenica Wilkie

Printed in China

TO SAY YES, YOU HAVE TO SWEAT AND ROLL UP YOUR SLEEVES AND PLUNGE BOTH HANDS INTO LIFE UP TO THE ELBOWS.

—JEAN ANOUILH

ONE CAN MAKE A
DAY OF ANY SIZE
AND REGULATE
THE RISING AND
THE SETTING
OF HIS OWN SUN
AND THE —JOHN MUIR
BRIGHTNESS OF
ITS SHINING.

IF YOU WANT TO BUILD A SHIP, DON'T DRUM UP THE MEN TO GATHER WOOD, DIVIDE THE WORK, AND GIVE ORDERS. INSTEAD, TEACH THEM TO YEARN FOR THE VAST AND ENDLESS SEA.

—ANTOINE DE SAINT-EXUPERY

dream

THINGS ARE ONLY IMPOSSIBLE UNTIL THEY'RE NOT.

—JEAN-LUC PICARD

smarts

IN THE SMALL MATTERS
—SIGMUND FREUD
TRUST THE MIND, IN THE LARGE ONES THE HEART...

THE HAPPIEST EXCITEMENT IN LIFE IS TO BE CONVINCED THAT ONE IS FIGHTING FOR ALL ONE IS WORTH ON BEHALF OF SOME CLEARLY SEEN AND DEEPLY FELT GOOD. —RUTH BENEDICT

DO NOT LET YOUR FIRE GO OUT,
SPARK BY IRREPLACEABLE
SPARK, IN THE HOPELESS —AYN RAND
SWAMPS OF THE APPROXIMATE,
THE NOT-QUITE, THE NOT-YET,
THE NOT-AT-ALL. DO NOT LET
THE HERO IN YOUR SOUL PERISH
IN LONELY FRUSTRATION FOR
THE LIFE YOU DESERVED, BUT
HAVE NEVER BEEN ABLE TO
REACH. CHECK YOUR ROAD AND
THE NATURE OF YOUR BATTLE.
THE WORLD YOU DESIRED CAN
BE WON. IT EXISTS, IT IS REAL,
IT IS POSSIBLE, IT IS YOURS.

WE ARE NOT GOING TO
SUCCEED IN EVERYTHING
WE ATTEMPT IN LIFE.
THAT'S A GUARANTEE.
IN FACT, THE MORE WE
DO IN LIFE, THE MORE
CHANCE THERE IS —SUSAN JEFFERS
NOT TO SUCCEED IN
SOME THINGS. BUT WHAT
A RICH LIFE WE ARE
HAVING! WIN OR LOSE,
WE JUST KEEP WINNING.

creativity

ALMOST ALL REALLY NEW IDEAS HAVE A CERTAIN ASPECT OF FOOLISHNESS WHEN THEY ARE FIRST PRODUCED. —ALFRED N. WHITEHEAD

language

EVER NOTICE THAT "WHAT THE HELL" IS ALWAYS THE RIGHT DECISION? —ROB ESTES

LEARNING TOO SOON OUR LIMITATIONS, WE NEVER LEARN OUR POWERS.

grateful.

—MIGNON MCLAUGHLIN

ORVILLE WRIGHT DIDN'T HAVE A PILOT'S LICENSE.

—RICHARD TAIT

WHEN EVERYONE AROUND YOU SAYS YOU CAN'T. WHEN EVERYTHING YOU KNOW SAYS YOU CAN'T. WHEN EVERYTHING WITHIN YOU SAYS YOU CAN'T. DIG DEEPER WITHIN YOURSELF, AND YOU FIND THAT YOU CAN. —MARK ELLIOT SACKS

perseverance

EVERY STRIKE BRINGS ME CLOSER TO THE NEXT HOME RUN.

—BABE RUTH

LIKE WATER, BE GENTLE AND STRONG. BE GENTLE ENOUGH TO FOLLOW THE NATURAL PATHS OF THE EARTH, AND STRONG ENOUGH TO RISE UP AND RESHAPE THE WORLD. —BRENDA PETERSON

OUR LIVES BEGIN TO END THE DAY WE BECOME SILENT ABOUT THINGS THAT MATTER.

—MARTIN LUTHER KING, JR.

ASK YOURSELF, "HOW LONG AM I GOING TO WORK TO MAKE MY DREAMS COME TRUE?" I SUGGEST YOU ANSWER, "AS LONG AS IT TAKES." —JIM ROHN

FOR ONCE YOU HAVE TASTED FLIGHT YOU WILL WALK THE EARTH WITH YOUR EYES —LEONARDO DA VINCI TURNED SKYWARDS, FOR THERE YOU HAVE BEEN AND THERE YOU WILL LONG TO RETURN.

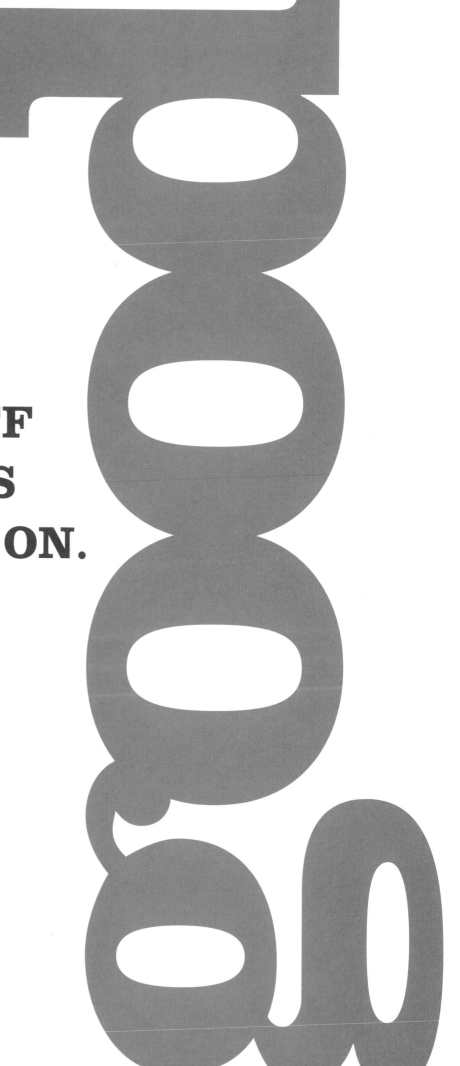

WE ARE SUCH STUFF AS DREAMS ARE MADE ON.

—WILLIAM SHAKESPEARE

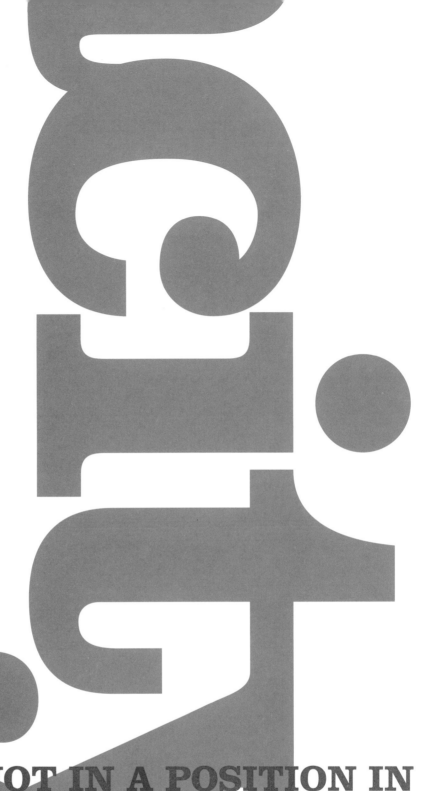

WE ARE NOT IN A POSITION IN WHICH WE HAVE NOTHING TO WORK WITH. WE ALREADY HAVE CAPACITIES, TALENTS, DIRECTION, MISSIONS, CALLINGS. —ABRAHAM MASLOW

THERE IS ALWAYS A CERTAIN PEACE IN BEING WHAT ONE IS, IN BEING THAT COMPLETELY. —UGO BETTI

excellence

WHAT YOU ARE WILL SHOW IN WHAT YOU DO.

—THOMAS A. EDISON

THERE ARE ONLY FOUR QUESTIONS WORTH ASKING: WHAT IS SACRED? OF WHAT IS THE SPIRIT MADE? WHAT IS WORTH LIVING FOR? WHAT IS WORTH DYING FOR? THE ANSWER TO ALL FOUR QUESTIONS IS THE SAME: ONLY LOVE. —DON JUAN DE MARCOS

esse

YOU DON'T HAVE A SOUL. YOU ARE A SOUL. YOU HAVE A BODY. —C.S. LEWIS

research

I'D RATHER BE A COULD-BE
IF I CANNOT BE AN ARE;
BECAUSE A COULD-BE IS A MAYBE
WHO IS REACHING FOR A STAR.
I'D RATHER BE A HAS-BEEN THAN
A MIGHT-HAVE-BEEN, BY FAR;
FOR A MIGHT-HAVE-BEEN HAS
NEVER BEEN,   —MILTON BERLE
BUT A HAS WAS ONCE AN ARE.

LET US GO SINGING AS FAR AS WE GO.

—VIRGIL